The Fight for Democracy

*The People's Movement Against a
Authoritarian Judicial System in Israel*

Hezekiah Israel

Table of contents

CHAPTER ONE

Protest in Israel

On Sunday night, protests broke out in Israel when prime leader Benjamin Netanyahu dismissed his defense minister Yoav Gallant for urging the suspension of contentious court reform and warned that it posed a threat to the country's security.

The controversy over the measures, which would severely curtail the judiciary's authority, has thrown Israel into a spiraling political crisis, alarmed investors, alarmed its allies, and sparked the largest wave of protests in more than a decade.

Following the announcement of Gallant's resignation on Sunday, additional protests broke out. Thousands of Israelis blocked the main road in Tel Aviv, while others engaged in physical altercations with police outside

Netanyahu's home in Jerusalem as the protests spread to more than 150 locations.

Israel's consul general in New York resigned in protest as the outrage grew, prompting a group of institutions to announce that they will begin a walkout on Monday morning.

Several responses to the outcry were heard inside the ruling coalition. Work on a portion of the court reform, according to one of its primary architects, will continue on Monday. If Netanyahu opted to halt the measures, three other ministers declared their support for him.

Gallant, the most senior member of Netanyahu's conservative administration, demanded a halt to the revamp on Saturday, warning that the division it had sparked was hurting the military. In opposition to the plans, thousands of reservists have vowed not to report for training.

Netanyahu opted to fire Gallant, his office announced in a terse statement less than 24 hours later. Following that, Netanyahu stated on Twitter: "We must stay firm in the face of anyone who refuses to serve."

Former Israeli military commander Gallant declared that maintaining the security of the nation "has always been and will always be my life's objective."

The coalition's simmering disagreements over the proposed amendments, which would give the government and its supporters greater control over the choice of judges while limiting the highest court's ability to overturn laws, were highlighted by Gallant's decision to break ranks.

The revisions, according to its proponents, are necessary to control an aggressive judiciary that has advanced a partisan leftist agenda.

Yet, detractors regard the reform as a serious threat to Israel's system of checks and balances that will weaken minority safeguards, encourage corruption, and hurt the country's economy.

The firing of Gallant was dubbed a "new low" for an "administration that threatens national security and defies the warning of all security officials" by Yair Lapid, leader of Yesh Atid, the main opposition organization.

He posted on Twitter, "Netanyahu can fire Gallant, but he cannot fire reality and the people of Israel who are defying the absurdity of the coalition.

Several opposition parties and former security personnel shared his criticism. Former air force commander Eitan Ben-Eliyahu claimed that Netanyahu had "called civil war."

The consul in New York, Asaf Zamir, stated that the revamp of the administration "undermines the entire premise of our democratic system" as he announced his retirement.

The events in Israel, which emphasize the urgent need for compromise, have prompted the Biden administration to express its "great concern," according to National Security Council spokesperson Adrienne Watson.

"We keep pressing the Israeli government to reach a deal as soon as feasible. For Israel and all of its residents, we think that is the wisest course of action, she said.

Hardliners in Netanyahu's alliance, though, rejoiced. The ultranationalist national security minister Itamar Ben-Gvir applauded Netanyahu after calling for Gallant to be fired following his statement on Saturday.

Whoever gives in to the military objectors cannot hold onto his position for even a single second, according to Ben-Gvir.

According to Netanyahu, the administration will move forward with the reform and submit the change to parliament for a final vote this week. The proposal will give the government more authority over judicial nominations.

But in the early hours of Monday, the ministers for the economy, the diaspora, and culture all declared that they would back Netanyahu if he opted to put off the change, signaling growing discomfort inside the coalition.

Nir Barkat, the economy minister, declared in a statement that "the reform is important and we will implement it." However, not at the cost of civil war.

Reservists, who play a significant role in the army's daily operations, including in senior units, have cautioned more frequently that they won't be able to serve in an undemocratic Israel under the government's plan.

Soldiers have expressed concern that a lack of international confidence in Israel's judiciary's independence could put them at risk of being tried in foreign courts for actions they were required to take while serving.

On Sunday morning, the PMO denied reports that Netanyahu had turned down Gallant's request to call the security cabinet together to discuss the security implications of the judicial reform, claiming that no such request had ever been made.

As the first significant indication of discontent inside the ruling coalition, Gallant joined those calling for the suspension of the parliamentary process for the judicial overhaul on Saturday night.

In a speech delivered live on television, Gallant stated, "I see the source of our strength eroding." "The IDF and security agencies are being affected by the widening rift in our society. The state's security is clear, right away, and tangibly threatened by this. I'm not going to help with this.

"The legislative process should be stopped now, for the sake of Israel's security, for the sake of our sons and daughters, so that the nation of Israel may celebrate Passover and Independence Day together, and may lament together on Memorial Day and Holocaust Remembrance Day," he said.

According to a senior defense source who spoke to reporters earlier on Sunday under the condition of anonymity, Israel's adversaries see the Jewish state as weak in light of the ongoing debate over the government's judicial reform.

The official claimed that Mossad leader David Barnea, Shin Bet head Ronen Bar, and military chief Herzi Halevi all agreed with him.

In the meantime, two Likud Knesset members who had hinted they could vote against some aspects of the government's judicial makeover changed their minds on Sunday and vowed to follow party policy, seemingly putting an end to an oncoming internal uprising.

Dichter, the agriculture minister who is reportedly being considered as Gallant's replacement, and rookie MK Eli Dallal both declared that they would support the various bills being pushed through the Knesset as part of the government's strategy to significantly curtail the judiciary's power and give the coalition near-total control over the appointment of judges.

Gallant's position received public endorsements from Likud MKs Yuli Edelstein and David Bitan, giving the opposition hope that a Likud uprising may prevent the coalition from passing the overhaul legislation.

Following the dismissal of the defense minister, Edelstein called a special, private meeting of the Foreign Affairs and Defense Committee of the Knesset, which he leads.

The committee announced that its members would meet with Gallant to talk about the "consequences of social tensions in Israel on the defense establishment."

The coalition will probably still have the necessary number of members to pass the bills based on Dichter and Dallal's statements, which serve as reminders of the loyalty Netanyahu can compel from allies even when under duress.

Dichter's decision to support the overhaul, which was widely perceived as a move to secure the defense minister post, drew intense criticism, and on Sunday night, protesters staged a demonstration in front of his Ashkelon home.

Yair Lapid, the leader of the opposition, criticized Netanyahu in response to Gallant's dismissal, calling it "a new low for an anti-Zionist government that is hurting national security and rejecting the warnings of all security figures."

He declared, "The Prime Minister of Israel is a danger to the State of Israel."

Benny Gantz, the leader of the National Unity party and Gallant's predecessor as defense minister declared that Israel's security is under "obvious, immediate, and physical threat."

"The threat has increased. This evening, Netanyahu prioritized politics and himself over security, according to Gantz.

Outside the residence of Agriculture Minister Avi Dichter in the southern coastal city of Ashkelon on March 26, 2023, Israelis demonstrated against the government's reform of the judiciary.

Avigdor Liberman, the leader of Yisrael Beytenu and a former defense minister, described the dismissal of Gallant by Netanyahu as "dictatorship at its best."

On Twitter, Liberman stated that the defense minister "dared to express the deep concern of all the heads of the security branches over the disintegration of the IDF and fatal harm to Israel's security."

"Netanyahu took the way of all dictators, stifling voices, instead of listening to [Gallant] and calling the cabinet."

Merav Michaeli, the head of the labor movement, claimed that the action proves Netanyahu "is very dangerous to Israel now, more than ever."

Former National Unity party justice minister Gideon Sa'ar referred to Gallant's dismissal as "an act of folly."

According to Sa'ar, there has never been a defense minister fired in Israel's history for issuing a warning about security risks as required by his position. Israel and its future are put at peril every day that Netanyahu is in office.

In a speech delivered Thursday night, Netanyahu declared that he would soften some aspects of the proposed shakeup moving forward amid widespread protests that had drawn hundreds of thousands of people into the streets.

He said, however, that the Knesset would vote on a bill in the coming days that would directly place the presidency of the Supreme Court and other important appointments under coalition control.

Although Tuesday has been suggested as a potential date for the vote, the exact time has not yet been determined.

On Sunday morning, the Knesset Constitution, Law, and Justice Committee met to continue drafting and passing the law in preparation for its second and third (and final) readings in the Knesset.

The appointments measure has been declared unconstitutional by the overhaul's opponents, who claim it will seriously undermine Israel's democratic character and politicize the judiciary.

CHAPTER 2

Elements of the Planned Overhaul in Israel

After Benjamin Netanyahu was sworn in as prime minister to head Israel's 37th government in late December 2022, his cabinet set out right away to introduce several laws that would allow several ministers—including Netanyahu, who would not be removed from office, and Arie Deri, who would be seated as a minister—to ensure their continued participation in the government.

In recent years, both of them have encountered legal issues. More generally, Netanyahu's Likud-led coalition immediately proposed a significant reform of Israel's judicial appointment procedure intending to give the parliament, or Knesset, the ultimate say in how judges would be chosen going forward.

The overhaul's obvious goal was to weaken the authority of judges and the Israeli judicial system, giving the ruling coalition more control over future laws and essentially eliminating the ability of courts, and particularly the Supreme Court, to overturn laws that might otherwise be seen as being in opposition to the coalition's political views.

The overhaul's goal was to politicize the judiciary; the legislation attempted to do away with the court's role as a check on the Knesset's legislative agenda.

A change of this kind would make it impossible for the Supreme Court, for instance, to declare a Knesset law to be "unconstitutional." Israel does not have a formal constitution, but it does have fundamental laws that the court has deemed to be the benchmark for rights and civil liberties in Israel through precedent.

The Israeli public erupted into the streets in civil protest after the proposed laws were presented to the Knesset in January 2023.

They were enraged by the idea that the Knesset might transform into an autocratic body. The demonstrations lasted for at least ten weeks straight and were essentially nonstop.

The Israeli media, friends of Israel abroad like Germany and France, foreign investors, Israeli military officials and reservists, and US executive and legislative officials, among others, all voiced opposition to the proposed legislation.

The potential economic ramifications that could befall Israel are most vividly illustrated in a ten-minute segment by the former president of the Bank of Hungary, Andras Simor.

Israeli President Isaac Herzog appealed to the ruling coalition to compromise in its plans to overhaul the judicial selection procedures and, in particular, to slow down in its haste to change the fundamental nature of Israel's democratic institutional system of "checks and balances" in two significant speeches to the nation on February 12, 2023, and March 9, 2023.

Prime Minister Netanyahu rejected the Israeli president's request for a compromise following Herzog's second appeal, but a number of the ideas considered in the judicial overhaul package were delayed or modified in the week of March 21.

Israel's Democracy Institute (IDI) identified the four components of the Netanyahu government's proposed overhaul of Israel's judiciary in January–February 2023 as follows:

- A provision is known as an "override clause" that limits judicial review of legislation.
- Changes to the composition of the Judicial Selection Committee to guarantee that government appointment to the bench is under control.
- Revocation of the Supreme Court's "standard of extreme unreasonableness" for interfering with executive directives.
- The conversion of legal advisers to ministers into political appointees.

CHAPTER 3

Israel's judicial overhaul: What is the coalition planning and where does it stand?

The coalition hopes to finish the plan within a month. It will give politicians the authority to appoint judges and prevent courts from reviewing nearly all legislation and ministerial appointments.

The government of Prime Minister Benjamin Netanyahu is working quickly to pass an ambitious, comprehensive plan to stifle the judiciary and assert unheard-of political power.

The Supreme Court, which also serves as the High Court of Justice, is essentially no longer able to serve as a check on the Knesset and the ruling coalition, according to critics, who claim that this represents a revolutionary change in Israeli governance.

According to experts, this could transform Israel from a liberal democracy to another form of government.

Critics draw attention to the threat it poses to liberal democratic institutions, the rule of law, and the safeguards for civil liberties in addition to the economic, diplomatic, and legal repercussions that experts and world leaders have already hinted at.

Proponents of the overhaul have dismissed large-scale demonstrations and requests to halt the legislative effort.

To "strengthen democracy," those who support the package of bills that make up the plan argue that power needs to be "rebalanced" away from an activist judiciary and toward the people's elected representatives.

They claim that many people in their group do not support the court, which has long been regarded as a stronghold of liberalism, and instead want to increase social and ideological diversity within its ranks.

The overhaul's creator and ardent ideologue, Justice Minister Yariv Levin, has declared he will continue advancing it quickly. The rollout is currently on track to be finished before the Knesset's April 2 recess for Passover.

While opposition members and President Isaac Herzog have both set freezing the process as a condition for discussion, to avoid giving a fig leaf for an overhaul that will proceed unchanged, Levin has stated that he is open to dialogue as the legislation moves toward becoming law.

Amid eight weeks of escalating protest, a small group of MKs from Benny Gantz's National Unity party and Levin's Likud published an open letter on Wednesday inviting both parties to the negotiating table—again, without addressing the issue of preconditions.

In Tel Aviv, mounted police move against protesters opposing the government's proposed judicial reform.

The main elements of the ongoing judicial upheaval are outlined below, along with an explanation of where each stands in the legislative process.

What it entails to put political control over judicial appointments

This component would change the makeup of the nine-member Judicial Selection Committee and lower the number of votes needed to install a judge to five, giving the coalition complete power over the nomination of judges.

Coalition lawmakers would hold the same number of committee members.

The Judicial Selection Committee currently strikes a balance between political and professional interests by the division of panel membership and by needing seven of the nine members to agree before choosing a Supreme Court justice, forcing compromise between the groups. Judges at lower courts, however, simply need five votes.

The new panel will shift seats to eliminate the Israel Bar Association and give three seats to ministers and three seats to MKs, replacing its current composition of three judges, two IBA representatives, and four politicians.

Instead of all three seats being filled by Supreme Court justices, the justice minister may select two extra judges, including from lower courts, with the president's consent.

The administration may select two more ministers for the panel, in addition to the justice minister. The Knesset speaker will also choose one additional coalition legislator, the chairman of the Constitution, Law, and Justice Committee, and a third MK from the opposition.

Supporters claim that many Israelis do not view the Supreme Court as a representative of their nation and that the court's 15 justices do not reflect the values or identities they embrace.

Politicians contend that by putting appointments under political control, coalition politicians who were chosen by the people will be able to produce a court that is more representative of their political parties.

Levin said the reform in the judicial selection panel will "allow pluralism," draw "judges from various sectors of the nation" and protect judicial independence as he celebrated the bill's passing its first Knesset vote in late February.

The Supreme Court and the professional attorneys' group are accused of conspiring to use their influence to advance cronies, a charge that has been partially addressed by boosting the majority required to choose a judge from five to seven of the panel's nine votes.

What detractors claim: Detractors claim that the proposal will ultimately make the entire Supreme Court subservient to political parties in coalitions, giving them the authority to choose any candidate without having to reach an agreement with other justices.

Politicians will politicize the court and endanger its independence if they have sole discretion over judge selection and elevation.

Former justice minister Gideon Sa'ar has warned that lower court rulings may be made to win future promotions and that judges will know which politician they "owe" their seats to.

In Sa'ar's words, eventually, the entire Supreme Court will "owe" its seats to particular politicians or political parties.

The current state of the law: The bill to alter the court's makeup was supported by the Constitution, Law, and Justice Committee, and on February 21, it passed beyond its first reading and was sent back to the committee in anticipation of its second and third readings before becoming law.

Definition of preemptive immunity for legislation

The measure would prevent courts from overturning ordinary laws passed by the Knesset, provided that the legislation has an immunity clause specifically indicating that it cannot be contested because it violates a Basic Law, which is how courts have previously invalidated laws.

Not just a simple majority, but at least 61 MKs must approve the law for it to become law.

The protections of the clause may also be decided to be extended "indefinitely" by the next Knesset.

The clause would be in effect for the duration of the Knesset that passes it as well as for one year beyond that.

This section can also be added retroactively by amending existing law to include the measure, as Israeli law is easily altered through the same parliamentary process that is necessary for enacting a new law.

The immunity clause would not apply to those laws that need to be modified with a supermajority of 61 MKs or more.

Because it specifically indicates that the legislation is "legal, notwithstanding what is written in Basic Laws," the protective phrase is frequently referred to as a **"notwithstanding clause**."

The preventative step is part of a multifaceted effort to end High Court scrutiny of legislation, along with draft legislation that would restrict the Bench's authority and give the Knesset the power to reenact laws that have already been knocked down by the courts.

Supporters assert that the law "restores control to the people as the sovereign" through the Knesset, the people's representative.

They applaud the law for limiting court overreach as well. Several defenders claim that an aggressive High Court has made decisions that they disagree with, such as those that restrict illegal settlement activities and prevent the codification of extensive religious study exemptions from military service.

Chair of the Constitution Committee MK Simcha Rothman also asserted that it would be challenging to overcome the court's right to undertake judicial review due to the necessity to reach 61 MKs and built-in expiration.

The "notwithstanding clause," which lawmakers could include in almost any measure, prevents courts from considering legislation even if it directly conflicts with one of Israel's quasi-constitutional Basic Laws, according to critics.

Due to the lack of any other legal recourse outside of the legislative process, this might give Knesset members complete freedom to implement laws that restrict minority rights that are often guaranteed by the Basic Laws.

The current state of the law: This is being advanced through two parallel pieces of legislation, which Rothman's office refers to as a "technical" issue.

The first, a Rothman-sponsored private member's bill, passed its first reading on February 22. The measure is also being advanced by a second, concurrent Constitution Committee bill, which was given preliminary approval for the first reading by the committee on March 1.

limiting the court's interpretation of fundamental laws, especially it is capacity to uphold civil liberties

The measure's requirements: According to the proposed legislation, the High Court of Justice would only have the authority to invalidate Knesset bills if they "clearly" contravene a rule that is "entrenched" in a Basic Law.

This practically means that the High Court cannot infer civil liberties protections from Fundamental Laws unless those rights are specifically stated.

Fundamental civil rights, such as the right to equality and freedom of expression, are not explicitly stated in any Basic Laws, but they have nonetheless been incorporated into the fabric of Israeli law as a result of High Court decisions interpreting the Basic Laws, particularly Basic Law: Human

Dignity and Liberty. These rights would no longer be shielded from political change.

What proponents say: If the Basic Laws have the status of a constitution, then judges should interpret the legislation strictly and not try to wriggle rights out of the statute.

The supporter of this clause, Rothman, has maintained that if the High Court is permitted to invalidate legislation because the Knesset restricted its legislative authority through the Basic Laws, it may only do so under what is expressly stated in those laws.

The politician claimed that because of unspoken cultural agreements on the subject, civil freedoms would be protected.

After this legislation is passed, Rothman added that it is "possible" that the High Court may still hear cases regarding civil liberties that were obtained through the court system.

Proponents further claim that by defining what the court can and cannot review, the measure enshrines for the first time the authority to overturn laws, which was previously established by the court itself but never officially stated in the law.

What detractors claim: By depriving the court of this interpretation authority, the constitution's guarantee of civil freedoms is eliminated.

Gur Bligh, a legal advisor to the Constitution Committee, forewarned Rothman that there would be no constitutional protection for fundamental rights like freedom of speech if the court lost its jurisdiction to overturn laws that violated civil liberties that it had previously established.

The current state of the law: This provision is a component of two simultaneous laws that are related to the notwithstanding clause. On February 22, One, supported by Rothman, passed its initial reading. The Constitution Committee's second bill received preliminary approval from the committee on March 1 for its first reading.

What It Means to Prevent the Supreme Court From Reviewing Fundamental Legislation?

The Fundamental Laws cannot be subject to Supreme Court regulation.

Supporters claim that Basic Laws have quasi-constitutional status and should be shielded from judicial review.

What detractors say: Basic Laws are granted unique standing, but typically not a special process. They are intended to constitute the draft chapters of a future Israeli constitution.

Most Basic Laws are easily amenable with a simple majority of MKs present and voting, and they can be used to support failed rotation agreements between Netanyahu and National Unity leader Benny Gantz or to address other pressing political issues.

The coalition, according to critics, is attempting to have it both ways by treating the Basic Laws as both constitutional and highly changeable.

They point out that Rothman declared the Basic Laws were not a constitution at the beginning of his committee's first reading.

Critics also draw attention to the fact that the legislation preventing Basic Law review is an addition to Basic Law: The Judiciary would be exempt from the final legislation.

The bill, which is a part of the Judicial Selection Committee reform package, passed its first reading on February 20 and is currently being discussed in Rothman's committee in preparation for second and third readings.

Larger Panels and Thresholds are Required for Judicial Review

What the proposal requires is that 12 of the current 15 Supreme Court justices, or 80% of them, must agree to overturn a law. It will be necessary to impanel the whole 15-justice bench during hearings in which a statute is being reviewed.

Supporters complain that laws are too readily overturned by the High Court, which at the moment only requires a simple majority in a panel of 9 or 11 justices to do so.

The court has annulled 22 statutes in whole or in part since it established its substantive judicial review authority in 1995.

What detractors say: Raising the bar to 12 of the 15 justices on the court will make it exceedingly challenging to invalidate laws given the ideological variety on the bench.

The court would find it challenging to carry out any significant substantive judicial review when combined with other proposals to restrict the court's monitoring of laws, such as eliminating Basic Law review and enacting a preemptive immunity clause.

Yet, they object to the unusually high standard that is set by this proposal. Many opponents of judicial reform are amenable to raising the threshold for invalidating legislation.

Bligh, a legal advisor to the Constitution Committee, backed up this critique by noting that almost any other democracies have a specific majority requirement for judicial review.

The law was temporarily passed on March 1 for its first reading in the Knesset by the Constitution, Law and Justice Committee, which sponsored it; however, it will return to the committee on March 5 for a second vote to override objections.

A companion private member's bill that passed its first reading on February 22 contains identical legislation.

Defending the prime minister from being compelled to take a leave of absence

The bill only provides for two possible methods for a prime minister to resign from office: either the premier notifies the Knesset that they are doing so, or three-quarters of cabinet members vote to place the premier on leave of absence, which must then be approved by at least 90 Knesset members. Recusal must be justified by physical or mental incapacity.

The legislation also states that no court shall have the authority to consider or rule on a petition calling for the prime minister's resignation.

A petition asking the High Court of Justice to require Netanyahu to withdraw himself due to his perceived conflict of interest in overseeing significant legal and judicial reforms while he is himself facing corruption charges was granted hearing last month.

On March 2, Netanyahu's legal team informed the High Court that the attorney general's claim that the premier would have a conflict of interest if he participated in judicial reform policies was "theoretical, conjecture."

Supporters' arguments: According to bill sponsor Ofir Katz (Likud), the prime minister is chosen by the people and their representatives, and the judiciary shouldn't become involved.

The plan would drastically decrease the circumstances under which a prime minister may be required to recuse himself or herself, according to Attorney General Gali Baharav-Miara, who has stated that she opposes it and warns that it would create a legal "black hole."

The current state of the law: On March 1, the measure passed its preliminary reading in the Knesset and is now anticipated to go to a new committee under the direction of Katz for work on its first reading.

'Deri 2': Removing Court Discretionary Control Over Ministerial Appointments

The measure's requirements: The law prohibits the High Court of Justice from examining ministerial appointments unless they directly contravene the Basic Law's fitness standards: governmental body.

The new legislation, known as "Deri 2," is specifically intended to bring Shas leader Aryeh Deri back into the cabinet.

Deri received a suspended sentence as part of a plea agreement despite being found guilty of tax violations last year. The emerging coalition passed an amendment to Basic Law: The Government in December to make it clear that only appointees who were sentenced to custodial prison sentences would be subject to the turpitude test.

This was done out of concern that the suspended sentence could still carry a "moral turpitude" ruling that would require Deri to take a seven-year break from politics.

The High Court of Justice, however, declared in January that Deri's accession to the government was "very irrational" and banned by estoppel because it was asserted that he promised to leave politics in the January 2022 plea agreement.

So, Netanyahu's key ally was fired by order of the attorney general.

Supporters argue that the courts shouldn't stifle the voice of the people, who elected lawmakers and brought them to the Knesset and the government with their ballots. Politicians claim that removing the Shas leader will invalidate the ballots of about 400,000 people who supported Shas in the previous election.

Critics claim that this is an individualized attempt to re-elect Deri by altering the game's rules in the middle.

The current state of the law: Moshe Arbel, a Shas MK, introduced the private member's bill, which passed its first reading on February 22 and started the discussion in a select committee on March 1.

excluding the State Attorney's Office from oversight of police internal investigations
The measure's requirements: The idea would hand over the responsibility of the Police Internal Investigations Department—currently under the State Attorney's Office—so that the Justice

Minister could use it to look into state attorneys.

This indicates that political control will replace the unit's previous autonomous, professional authority within the Justice Ministry.

Supporters' comments: Former deputy head of the internal investigations unit and disgruntled Likud MK Moshe Saada claims the transfer will avoid conflicts of interest because the State Attorney's Office and police frequently collaborate, making it difficult for them to maintain independent investigations.

What the critics are saying: According to the critics, this amendment would give the Justice Minister the authority to authorize police or prosecutor investigations against political allies. This issue is brought up against the background of the Likud's extensive efforts to attack the police and prosecutors for their investigation into and subsequent indictment of Netanyahu in three corruption cases.

Netanyahu is still facing charges but maintains his innocence. He says the accusations were made up by a state prosecution and police department that were motivated by politics and who received support from left-wing politicians and a leftist media. A weak attorney general also allowed this to happen.

The attempt to disband its police investigation unit has drawn criticism from the State Attorney's Office for eroding professionalism.

Currently, Saada's private member's bill, which passed its first reading on February 22, is being prepared for committee consideration.

The coalition has also indicated other reforms

The plenum is yet to be presented with some other components of the planned judicial reform. The following are some of them.

Changing legal advisors' roles from being professional authorities to being trusted advisors with discretion: Ministry legal advisers are currently professionally subordinate to the attorney general, preserving their independence.

Politicians who run ministries are constrained by their views. Legal counsel must also be provided for Ministries.

The bill, which has been submitted to the Constitution, Law, and Justice Committee but is now on hold, would allow ministers to choose their legal counsel and render the opinions of the attorney general and ministry counsel as well as ministers and the cabinet non-binding.

Additionally, the government would have the option of hiring attorneys of their choosing, giving them stronger support for whatever stances they take that are in opposition to official legal advice.

Reducing the judicial "reasonableness" test: Levin has advocated for the abolition of the judicial "reasonableness" test, which allows courts to assess and strike down irrational actions made by the public or private sector.

On the other side, Rothman suggests restricting the test's use to elected officials alone.

The most recent use of the reasonableness test was to argue against Deri's appointment to two ministerial positions in light of his most recent tax fraud conviction.

establishing an override clause, which allows the Knesset to reinstate laws that have been struck down by the courts: This law would give the Knesset the ability to re-legislate laws that had been ruled illegal by the court, serving as an alternative to preemptive immunity.

The precise number of lawmakers needed for such an override is still up for debate, but current suggestions range from giving the Knesset this authority with a majority of 61 MKs, as promoted by Levin, to an 80 MK supermajority, as put forth by Gantz.

Moving the selection of the Supreme Court's president and vice president to political control: Levin has proposed moving the selection of the court's president, who determines which justices and how many will handle cases, directly into politicians' hands rather than having the court make appointments based on seniority precedent.